WHOSE LIFE ARE YOU LIVING?

The journey to self-discovery

J. Barbier

ISBN: 1533365199
ISBN 13: 9781533365194
Library of Congress Control Number: 2016912659
CreateSpace Independent Publishing Platform
North Charleston, South Carolina

TABLE OF CONTENTS

CHAPTER 1

WHAT IS INSIDE OF YOU?

Your mind is like the ocean, and its water is knowledge. No matter how much you have, there is always room for more.

What is inside of you? No, I am not talking about physically, although that is also very important in living a great life. This book is about the mental aspects of life and the importance of feeding your mind healthy food. We all grow physically day by day, and we seem to assume that our mental growth follows the same law. But positive mental growth is intentional. Though you learn daily from what you see, hear, and do and through your parents, friends, and schooling, those learning platforms will only get you so far. The mental growth you need to set yourself above the crowd must be done intentionally, and this requires you to step outside the box that most people spend their lives in. I wrote this book to help you do just that.

The growth and knowledge required for a successful life, whether in a personal or professional sense, necessitates initiative from you. Let's keep it simple: if you want to learn to bake pies, it does not matter how big you've grown physically; you will not successfully bake pies unless you take the initiative to learn how. Replace "bake pies" with whatever else you desire, for it follows the same law.

I consider this book to be like a meal. After you read it (and are hopefully inspired by it and had your mind fed with knowledge), do you never need to eat again (or read the book again)? Can you only eat once and be full for the rest of your life? The obvious answer is no. I compare learning to food because it acts like food. One serving will not feed your stomach forever, and learning and feeding your mind is a daily task as well.

Why is it important to feed your mind? Unlike with physical hunger, your mind can't *stay* hungry. It will eat, regardless of whether you feed it—or something else does. Feeding your mind is not what is crucial; selecting what your mind gets fed is the key. If you do not eat today, your body will be hungry. But if you don't control what goes into your mind, it will feed on anything and everything around it. I picture my mind as the ocean. As big as the ocean is, new water constantly flows into it. Your mind is like the ocean. Knowledge, whether selected or random, is constantly flowing into it. It is up to you to control what gets in and stays in and what has to leave, or what you do not allow entry in the first place. In other words, as strange as it may seem, you need to control what type of water flows into your ocean.

Trash (as I like to refer to some things) is all around you. The second you wake up, you can pick up your phone and check Facebook, Instagram, Snapchat, your e-mail, and the news without even getting out of bed. Now don't get me wrong, those digital outlets aren't necessarily trash, but let's be honest. Most of the time, drama is all over social media sites, and the news is nothing but negative stories. Whether you are aware of it or not, your mind has its mouth wide open, feeding on all that information. If you begin your day that way, then it is already destined for negativity before you even brush your teeth.

I have often read that how you start your morning affects the rest of your day, and based on personal experiences, I agree. Imagine waking up, the earlier the better, and picking up your phone to read a motivational quote (or a Bible verse, if you are religious). Imagine listening to or reading something positive before going to work or school. I can guarantee that you will see a difference in your attitude and your mind-set. On most days, I read a Bible verse and then listen to a motivational speech for at least an hour—usually in the morning, but sometimes during the afternoon. I choose what my mind gets to eat way before I even think about my stomach or going out there to start my day. A good start to your day is only the beginning, and many would agree that it is crucial.

Now most of us, if we can help it, like to eat several times a day—at least three, on average. Personally, I like to eat six times a day. I love food. But over the years, I have developed an even bigger appetite for knowledge. I feed my mind more times daily than I can count. Most of us feed our stomachs more than we feed our minds. We would rather spend money at a nice restaurant than spend time gaining knowledge at a free library. Most of us also settle for what we can get in life, not what we truly desire—we're not living the lives we constantly dream of.

When it comes to feeding your mind, feeding it several times a day is a must. Once a day by far is not enough and will not help you maintain a healthy mind. The great thing about feeding your mind is how inexpensive it can be. Search YouTube for motivational speeches or whatever area you feel a need to improve on, and countless videos will come up—same scenario with Google. These outlets alone are two of the best tools that you can use to grow your mind for free. YouTube is by far my favorite. It contains countless audio clips as well as videos of just about anything that we all can learn from. The most educational videos are not on the front page, since they are not superpopular, but that is what is great about them. You are not aiming just to be part of the crowd. If you wish to be among the select few who create their lives every day, then you have to start by studying what they do. Then just simply follow in their footsteps.

You know that I start my morning with positive messages. My favorite speaker to listen to is Les Brown. If you are not familiar with that name, I suggest you immediately put this book down and search YouTube for him. (I'll say more about Brown later.)

Next on my schedule is a gym session. I'm what you would call a gym rat—I live and breathe fitness. Driving there, I have an audiobook playing, rarely music. When I am working out and my physical body is in pain, and I'm ready to cry and quit, my iPod is playing motivational speeches, pushing me beyond my physical limits. So within hours of waking up, I have already selected more of what to feed my mind than most people do in a week. From there on, I spend most of my driving time learning from audiobooks on different subjects such as business, sales, mind-set, positive thinking…you can say I'm a self-help book junkie and proud of it. Close your eyes and see the words with your mind: I am a big visual thinker. Your mind has the power to create anything you can think of, so why not use it? But to create with your mind beyond what you see with your eyes, you need to know how.

Let's play a guessing game. Person One wakes up and watches the news: murder, a shooting, global warming, war, a cop killed a kid, a drunk driver killed someone—you name it, all the garbage you can think of gets sucked right into his mind. He goes out driving, and someone cuts him off. How do you think he reacts? After all, according to the news, the world is a war zone. Person Two wakes up and reads something positive, spiritual, and motivating about the power of forgiveness, counting your blessings, and being patient. He goes out driving, and someone cuts him off. How do you think he reacts or responds?

Is Person Two perfect? Of course not. But I would bet on him to handle the situation in a more positive manner compared to Person One. After all, your actions and words are a direct result of what is in your mind and heart.

Since I started the journey toward a positive and mentally strong mind-set, I have been cut off by drivers countless times and experienced similar such events, and I usually manage to respond in a positive manner. For example, I focus more on the blessing that my car did not get hit and that I still have my health. I have been on the other side, where I have cut people off—and they immediately react with anger instead of responding with compassion. It is not about being better than others; it is about being better for you. Your thought process and reaction will have an effect on you. The more negative you are, the more poison you have inside of you. You are 100 percent in charge of your actions and reactions. If someone betrays you in any way and then you betray them, your actions are still your own to take responsibility for. Think about it. Fighting fire with fire only results in both parties losing; it's just that one may lose more than the other. Your words, your actions, and your thoughts are reflections of the seeds you have growing inside of your mind.

Let's move on to the bigger picture: your life itself. Where you are right now in life is the result of the knowledge and wisdom you have possessed in your mind and the courage you have had in your heart. Your physical body has next to nothing to do with it. Now, ladies and gents, I am not blind to a few facts. Yes, if you want to be an NBA basketball player, a certain height helps, although a few have broken that rule. If you want to play football, size will play a part, but that rule has also been broken. These rules are really just obstacles you will need to overcome. Now this is where the mind comes into play. Say you are five feet tall and you want to play in the NBA. Chances are that you will not make it on the court. But where else can your mind take you? How many coaches are in the NBA that have never been players? How many referees? There are countless other opportunities in the NBA that do not require basketball-playing skills.

Your mind will take you beyond what your eyes see. If you truly love basketball, have a passion for it, and are willing to devote your life to being part of the game, you will without a doubt find a way to get into the NBA. Whatever you wish to accomplish, it is the same process. Let's say you want to be an actor. In my opinion, that career is possible for anyone. The people you see on the screen are large and small; white, Hispanic, black, and Asian; male and female; skinny and fit—the list goes on. If you want to be an actor, chances are, there's a place in Hollywood for you. Yes, it's easier said than done. And if you are not feeding your mind with food that helps you grow and overcome any obstacles, getting you to think outside the box, then you will always live by the means that are available right in front of you.

Investing in yourself is the greatest thing you will ever do for your family and the world, for you are the greatest asset you will ever have. Why do we spend more time watching TV, playing video games, and going out than we do reading books, going to seminars, or going to school? Why do people choose to work five days a week at jobs they are not happy with, only to have the weekend as a reward and possibly to retire at sixty-five?

We say, "Thank God it's Friday," as if it is not possible to say, "Thank God it's Monday" (or Tuesday or Wednesday or Thursday). Monday is not your enemy. Your lack of ability, desire, passion, and motivation is. Stop being mad and depressed on Mondays. Be mad at yourself for that, and then take action to change your situation. Whether you like it or not, as long as you're breathing Mondays will be a part of your life. So why not figure out how to enjoy them; how to cry tears of joy and thank God because it is Monday.

We seem to think that enjoying every day of one's life is reserved only for the few, those people on TV we look up to—actors, athletes, your favorite singer, multimillionaires and billionaires. We wish to accomplish and live similar lifestyles as those we admire— as do I—but all most people do is wish and wish. Few of us take action, and even fewer keep going after rejections, failures, and barely being able to eat in the process, but those few usually end up breaking through.

What is the difference between those who break through and those who don't even start the race to achieving their goals and live the lives they want to live? It is mind-set. The world is available to us—all the opportunities, the happiness, the wealth—it is all around us. But it will take more than what your eyes can see to obtain your share of it. Your mind needs to become your main source of sight, for only your mind can see what is possible in your future. Close your eyes and open your mind to having a billion dollars in the bank. Where do you see yourself? What are you wearing? Driving? Where are you traveling to? Are you still mad about Monday? Probably not, right? Your mind just turned you into a billionaire for a few seconds.

Do you want to be a billionaire? Do you want to be a CEO? If you want to be a billionaire, it's possible…look at the founders of Facebook, GoPro, or 5-hour Energy. You need to start thinking and taking action like one, then—because knowing is only half the battle. We must also believe in our ability to go out in this challenging world and apply our knowledge. It is not possible to think like a billionaire if you are not following the billionaire path. It includes working on the mind more than working on watching TV, playing video games, going to clubs, and talking about other people's lives.

Bill Gates, founder of Microsoft, the billion-dollar company that produces the Xbox gaming system, probably has never played an Xbox. Yet at every purchase of one, money goes to his bank account. As rich as he is, he reads about fifty books a year. You're behind on your bills, avoiding phone calls from collectors, but somehow manage to get enough money together for a gaming system to play video games as an escape for a few hours. Yet how many of the masses out there who are struggling to make ends meet have

never thought of visiting the local free library to gain the knowledge to escape the rat race and have complete freedom and control
over their lives? Bill Gates can wake up and never get out of bed at
this point. He will still make more money that day than most people do in a year or lifetime. Yet he reads. Keep that in mind. Now if
you are saying to yourself that Bill Gates is a supergenius and that's
how he has been able to reach the level he is at today, then I would
guess you have never read *Outliers* by Malcolm Gladwell, and you
probably have never heard of Christopher Langan either.

One of my favorite Norman Vincent Peale quotes is, "Shoot
for the moon. Even if you miss, you will land among the stars."
If you aim to be a billionaire and you fail, at worst you'll have a
few million in your account. And through your journey, you will
have gained experience and knowledge that even Harvard will not
teach you. Truth be told, a college degree does not equal a successful and happy life. If you study millionaires and billionaires, you'll
find that quite a few of them do not have college degrees.

What is inside of you? What has your mind been feeding on your
whole life? What have you been aiming for? Have you been making decisions based on what your eyes see, or has your mind played
a part in it? You're a farmer, cultivating your mind. What kind of
crops have you been planting? The crops you are giving to the world
are a result of the seeds you have planted in your mind. If you want
something different, you need to start with you. Start taking better
care of your soil, and select the seeds you would like to grow instead
of letting the outside world do it for you. Watch your crops, and take
care of them daily. You will not see results today; neither are you
guaranteed results tomorrow. But I can assure you that if you keep
growing your mind and your heart, your life will grow.

Most people like to see the light at the end of the tunnel before
committing to going in. Well, I can guarantee that if you can immediately see the light, it is a very short tunnel and is usually the
easier way out and available for everyone to travel through. How

hard is it to fill out a job application? It is easier to make a decision to work at a job you hate, knowing there's a paycheck at the end of the week, than to pursue your dream and not know when (or if) that first check will come. It is much harder to spend your free time reading, studying, building, taking action, falling on your face over and over and over again, and being the only one who believes in you. Yes, that is a long tunnel with no light in sight. But, ladies and gents, at the end of the tunnel is where the few get to wake up and live life to the fullest.

Your life will forever be the product of your mind. Even if you win the lottery, that money has the power to fly away faster than it came. Just because you stumble on money does not mean you also have the knowledge to manage it. The people who have made it to the end of the long tunnel are not wishing for heaven. They are not cursing Mondays. They probably don't even like to sleep—why should they? Their actual lives are more pleasurable than dreaming. Those people exist all around the world, all around us today. Some of those people were born lucky, I suppose…imagine calling Bill Gates "Dad." But many of them were just where you and I are now. However, they made a decision that this would not be it. They gained the knowledge and developed the mind-set to understand that their current situation was just that—current—and that, by any means necessary and without breaking human law, they would reach the end of the long tunnel and live the lives they always dreamed of. If you can dream it, you can achieve it. You are not capable of dreaming of anything your mind has never been exposed to. It starts with feeding your mind with the right knowledge. The bigger your mind is, the bigger your vision and success will be. The world and your circumstances are what they are, so if you desire to change them, you must change you.

CHAPTER 2
OCEAN OF WEALTH

Feed Your Mind the Things You Want as Your Reality

Wealth is like the ocean. Have you ever thought that? Well, think about it now. The ocean has been around since… well, I am not a scientist, but I know that it has been around for millions of years. Yet when was the last time you heard about any kind of conflict over ocean water or any talk of ocean water shortages? The point is, there is enough ocean water for all of us to enjoy, the same way that there is enough wealth on the planet for all of us to share. Now I am sure that at this point in your life, you already know that wealth is not as easily obtainable as ocean water in most cases. I say "most" because a few get lucky and win the lotto or have the privilege of calling billionaires their parents, but those are rare cases. Let's focus on the mass population and how to get out of the rat race.

Wealth has been around for thousands of years, the same way the ocean has. People become new millionaires and even billionaires every year. Again, let's keep the lucky few out of the equation and focus on the masses. I imagine that most new millionaires did not simply wake up, work a nine-to-five job, save in a 401(k), and make their millions that way. But the truth is, most people are following that "work and save for the future" path today. Do you honestly believe that a miracle will happen and you will not end up like most people in the category with that plan? I think not. You must plan for success and freedom. They will not happen by you simply growing older or by the government changing. All the tools that you need to accomplish dreams beyond your imagination are here on earth at your disposal for the most part, but faith and action will be required from you. Wishful thinking gives you hope, prayers give you faith, and action gives you the result. Remember, it is not easy, but always keep it simple. You don't obtain success by trying to conquer everything at once. Simply aim to conquer every second of every minute of every hour of every day of every week of every month, every year of your life.

There are people who are five or ten (or more) years older than you who are doing, at best, average in life. How do you think they ended up in that position? And how can you avoid being there yourself in the future? You have to remember that the old man who can barely afford his cell phone bill was once a young man. And just like the ocean was around when he was young, so were wealth, freedom, and happiness. Again, wealth, for the most part, is not going to run up and sit on your lap. You have to run toward it.

Your life is your life. Always take full responsibility for every aspect of it. Everything that you do not have at this point is because of everything you are not. We get what we are, not what we want. You have heard this a thousand times, but it needs to be mentioned a million more. So many out there still do not understand the fact that if you want to change any area of your life, then *you* must change. An external change in anything is temporary. Permanent change must always come from within, for who you are will equal the results that you produce.

Search the Internet for new billionaires and millionaires in the last ten years. I would guess that some are athletes, actors, singers, and so on. We are not all blessed with talents like those, but the list of the new rich also includes business owners, investors, and inventors. You know, people like Mark Zuckerberg.

Why do I believe that wealth is like the ocean, with enough to go around? Within a few years, Mark Zuckerberg became one of the richest men in the world. Where did that fortune come from? He didn't discover gold. He simply discovered how to create a site that millions all over the world use for free that also offers a place for other companies to advertise. Becoming wealthy is not rocket science. Forget about coming up with a million-dollar idea and focus on coming up with an idea that millions of people could benefit from. The more people you are able to reach, the bigger your financial wealth will grow. Too often, we focus on making money instead of providing value. When you focus on making money first, your mind tends to get clouded, as if no idea is big or expensive enough to reach that million-dollar goal. When you focus on serving the people, then it becomes about passion, which is what will wake you up early in the morning and keep you up late at night. Focus on reaching people, and the money will come.

Millionaires are being made on a regular basis—young, old, black, white, gray, in America, in China—you name it, it is being done. So why is it that some work for a teaspoon of the ocean while others seem to have an endless supply? Well, they made a choice. One chose to work for a teaspoon; the other chose to own a piece of the ocean itself. In the countless books I have read and the many more audio programs I have listened to, not one of the stories involved someone working hard at a job, saving the traditional way, and becoming rich in the process. If you wish to become wealthy, then you need to study the people who have done it like you are studying for a master's degree. Remember, success leaves clues, and in this day and age, those clues are too easy to find. All you have to do is decide to look for them.

When people hear "wealth," they immediately picture money. Truthfully, money comes at the end of wealth, which is something I learned from one of the most famous books of all time: Napoleon Hill's *Think and Grow Rich*. Obtaining your share of the ocean is not all about money. Just like there are many species of fish in the sea, many aspects of life add up to true wealth. Money is the most common measure of wealth, although not the most important. Would you rather have both of your legs or a million dollars? What is a mansion worth if you are alone with no real loved ones to share it with? What's money if you are not healthy enough to enjoy it? Money alone will not bring you wealth and happiness. It sure does help, but true riches are created from within. When you seek wealth, seek all aspects of it. Money will only buy you things. In the words of Napoleon Hill, here is what constitutes wealth: "a positive mental attitude, sound physical health, harmony in human relations, freedom from fear, the hope of future achievement, the capacity for applied faith, willingness to share one's blessings with others, to be engaged in the labor of love, an open mind on all subjects toward all people, complete self-discipline, wisdom with which to understand people, financial security."

Have you ever told yourself you could not do something? "I'm not smart enough to be a lawyer. I don't have the skills to be an actor. I don't have the money to..." and so on. People don't realize the power of their words and how the difference between average and great accomplishments can literally be determined by choices of words. The word "can't," in my opinion, is one of the worst you can use. Tell yourself that you can't, and you will easily prove yourself right. Keep in mind that enough people already believe that you can't. You yourself cannot afford to be one of them.

I remember growing up and only wanting a way to get a teaspoon of the ocean—a big teaspoon, if that helps my case. I never once thought about owning a water pipeline. What is the price of dreaming big? Your imagination is completely free. But remember, you will not be able to imagine any more than the knowledge you possess in your mind. The ocean itself is not big enough for me. I want the whole universe—not to be selfish, but who's to judge my limit? I believe that I am the son of a God, and my father has no limit; therefore, I have no limits but the ones I allow people or my own self to set.

Ever wonder why so many people are unhappy with their jobs or careers, yet all they do is complain like someone is holding them hostage in their current position? About how they don't get paid enough and how the owner of the company is rich, but employees can barely pay bills? Maybe you are one of those people. I used to be. If you know where the money is, why complain about not being paid enough? What excuses can you come up with for not creating your own and instead accepting crumbs from someone else? How many people do you know who will wait hours in line for the newest iPhone and the new Jordans with no excuses but will not read a book even if you paid them to? Why is it so easy for people to wait in line and spend hundreds of dollars on shoes and electronics? It is one thing to waste money, but how can you afford to waste time? Once this second is gone, it is permanently gone, and you are now one step closer to dying. That statement is true for all living organisms.

Funny how that works, right? Wealth is like the ocean, but it is not easily obtained. Those with talent, such as singers and athletes, are already halfway to their ocean, but in most cases, getting to own your share of it is a long, painful, lonely journey. Hint: this is why very few are at the top and why so many settle for comfort instead of freedom.

I used to loathe Monday as if it were its fault that I did not enjoy the work that I was doing. Sadly, Monday did not care and kept showing up once a week, bright and early. Mondays are not going to change. But what you can change is what you do. Do something you love, and you and Monday (and every single day that

God blesses you with) are best friends. Recently, I watched a video on Facebook where a guy on a panel was talking to what seemed like board members about why he deserved to make fifteen dollars an hour working at a fast-food restaurant. The gentleman was extremely passionate. He loved what he did for a living and simply wanted to feed his family members and put a roof over their heads. I admire his stand and his passion, but by far, they are being wasted.

Let's be honest—fast-food franchises are designed as a system that can be run by monkeys; that is one key to their success. They have a strong system, but one that is simple to manage, thus making the business extremely simple to duplicate and run successfully. Should a person working at a fast-food restaurant earn more than someone with a college degree? Well, that is for you to judge. My goal here is simply to point to how we can all enjoy the American dream if we just aim for it. Why can't that gentleman take that same passion and motivation and achieve success beyond fifteen dollars an hour? I am sure he has his excuses, as we all do. But what you do beyond your excuses is the difference between the successful and the unsuccessful. If this gentleman took the same amount of time that he did to fight for fifteen dollars and read a book on success instead, he would probably be on a better road today. Let's face it, today it is a fight for fifteen dollars; tomorrow, it will be a fight for twenty dollars. People who are asking for more from others instead of themselves, waiting for handouts from the government, will always seek to ask for more in the future.

Begin to be aware of the words you think and speak. The more I learn, the more I realize how powerful the mind is and how crucial it is to keep negative thoughts and words out of it. Your mind has the power to make real what you think and speak of. I cannot be the only one who talks to himself (at least, I hope not). Sometimes I feel a little crazy with the amount of time I spend talking to myself. But it's really a great thing. You are with yourself 24–7, so who knows you better than you? Who is better to monitor you and/or hold you accountable than the self that is always with you? The voices inside your head are always running. The question is, who is in control of those voices, and which ones are you listening to?

All your reactions are the result of thoughts, no matter how quick the reactions. It is crucial that the right voices in your head are in charge. No one on earth is perfect; the bad thoughts will win sometimes, and your actions will reflect that. The quest is not to become perfect, but to improve and learn how to manage and control your thoughts every day. You've seen people talking and acting out of control—or maybe you've done it yourself. I know I have. The first thing I do after one of those rare moments is talk to myself. Talking to yourself means looking within, not to blame others but to take full responsibly and make necessary changes inside you first. Your poor actions, regardless of who else was involved, are still *your* poor actions.

What do you tend to talk to yourself about? For me, it's about self-improvement, never giving up when the dark hours arrive, taking care of my mom, and being financially free. I work from there. That you're reading this book is proof of what is possible once you make up your mind and commit yourself to getting the job done by any means necessary. I said to myself, "I will be a published author." Then I began to work on writing. Was it easy? No. Did I want to quit? Yes. But there is no better feeling than actually reaching a goal that you thought was unreachable.

My vision, my "why" for this book, is to reach millions, to feed people's minds the simple knowledge that could possibly be life changing. People talk about making the world a better place yet never take action on those words. I chose to make the world a better place, and I took action. There is nothing more special about me than about anyone else on this planet. Nobody is more special or better than you. You have the power within you to own as much of the ocean of life as you desire. Success is not reserved for only a few, but only a few are willing to travel down its harsh road. Most people would rather be comfortable and blame everything and everyone else for their shortcomings. Which road will you choose?

All humans are created equal. Allow no one to have power over you, not even the people you look up to. All of a sudden, I found myself looking up to people who did not fit who I had become. Why should I look up to someone? If I am looking up, then they must look down to see me and therefore have superiority and power over me. I simply admire and respect people's accomplishments. I respect what they have brought and keep bringing to the world. But human to human, we are equal. Again, allow no one to have power over you.

People forget that they are dying—as you are reading this book—and that time does not care about our feelings or failures. Time can either be your best friend or worst enemy; the choice is purely up to you. I make time my best friend by always moving with it. No matter what, I keep going because time doesn't stop for me, for you, or for the president of the United States. So when you fail, which you will, hang on to time and keep moving along with it. When you get rejected, remember that time will not stop to feel sorry for you, so you should not spend time feeling sorry for yourself either. The only option you have is to move with time. Even in success, I believe you still need to keep going with time, because there is always success after success. You can always improve yourself, your business, and your knowledge, and there is always room for improvement, just as there is always room for more water in the ocean.

The best way to defeat a feeling of failure and make the most of your time is to finish tasks, big or small. I know you have set out to accomplish a task or goal and actually finished it. It is an amazing feeling, especially if the road was challenging. But most people shy away from hard challenges, not realizing that we humans are powerful beyond measure. No one on earth can successfully predict all that you are capable of. Learn to face the hard challenges. The results and who you become in the process will amaze you.

The ability to wake up and create your life daily takes time. It has its challenges, and ups and downs and failures—or, should I say, lessons—are part of the journey. But, ladies and gents, it is simple. You will not enjoy every part of the process. I do not like to write, but how else can I produce a book if I do not put that feeling aside and focus on the bigger picture? I am not a fan of public speaking, but how can I be a motivational speaker if I act on that feeling? Keep it simple, and stick to your principles. Do what you need to do to reach your goals, no matter what your personal feelings are toward some of the tasks you must accomplish.

We live in a time where information on virtually any subject is a Google search away. Learning a skill, whether personal or business related, is as easy as watching a video on YouTube. Yet so many of us fail to learn some of the most common skills that have the power to make life richer in every sense of the word. Wealth is like the ocean? Well, so are love, hate, happiness, knowledge, and life lessons. Whatever you seek to achieve has already been done before. It is mind-blowing when people say they don't know where to start—as if they need to reinvent the wheel. One can almost say that there are no secrets to life, just things that we have not yet learned or know how to do. Most of us would like to make more money. Even Bill Gates still seeks to improve his company's profit. But most of us never take any risks or action. How much time do you spend studying the people who make the kind of money you wish for? Wishing will not get you anywhere. Learning and following the action steps are the only ways to create results. Keep it simple. If you are physically capable of doing something, then you are mentally capable of learning how. But the initiative to make it happen always starts with you.

Successful people I admire and respect usually have certain things in common. They are extremely positive, they started at the bottom, and each has a heartfelt story. And they wake up early—sometimes as early as 3:00 a.m. Yes, 3:00 a.m. People who are successful and have more money in the bank than they can count are waking up at 3:00 a.m.; meanwhile, you are behind on your bills and are waking up whenever, with no sense of time management. Of course, wanting money alone will not get you out of bed early. Plenty of people on this planet are in need of more capital, yet they sleep in on their days off. If you seek to be in the top 10 percent, then you need to start doing what the top 10 percent are doing right now. You must see yourself there; act as if you were already there way before you get there.

You will be the same person you are right now if someone just gave you a million dollars today. More only makes you more of what you already are. Do not wait for success to come for you to change. You will be waiting a long time. Change into who you seek to become, and success will follow. Yes, it is hard to wake up in the morning when your bank account is not reflecting what you want, but more sleep will not solve that issue. More action will. Keep it simple. The more you learn and the more you do, the more you will be who you seek to be, and the more success you will have. The world is yours for the taking.

CHAPTER 3

VISION

Before You Achieve It Physically, You Must First See It Mentally

Take a look around you. Look at what you wear, the vehicle you drive, and the house you live in. Look at anything around you at this moment. It's all *man-made*. You are literally living in countless people's imaginations, ideas, and dreams. The only difference between you and those who were able to turn their dreams into the reality you benefit from today is that they had enough courage to breathe life into their thoughts. If something is man-made, it started out as a thought, an idea, a vision. Where do those thoughts and ideas come from? Your imagination, your mind, your knowledge, and your wisdom. The power to imagine just about anything is one of the greatest gifts you possess. But as powerful as your imagination is, it has its limits: your knowledge and your ability to see and think beyond what you see with your eyes.

I often say that your eyes will make you blind. How is that possible? How can I believe and preach those words? In my many years of studying the subject of success, I have seen so many things in the world that were in front of me my whole life but that I was not capable of seeing before. Never in a million years did I think I would be sitting here writing a book, speaking on stage, being an entrepreneur, and more. I was looking at the world through only my eyes, and because of that, I only aimed for mediocre goals while being blind to countless opportunities that were right in front of me. Your eyes are not capable of seeing beyond what is currently in front of you. They are very limited and only have the power to show you the now.

If you are primarily using your eyes to see, then you are blind to a number of opportunities and future possibilities. You can only react to life instead of creating your life. The key is to see the now with your eyes and then transfer it to the mind for processing. We are all capable of achieving wondrous things, but everything falls back to the level of knowledge that you possess in your mind. Successful people build libraries in their mansions. They read a lot of books, attend seminars, and listen to audiobookshile they are driving. Plain and simple, they invest countless hours and dollars into improving their minds. Success in anything can actually be simple: the more you know and the more you apply and practice, the better you will be. That necessary knowledge most likely does not come to you while you're in front of the TV, hanging out with people, or going to clubs every week. Knowledge is like a healthy diet: it is not the most popular thing around, your peers most likely don't want to join you in it, and you may not like it at first. But once you start seeing changes in yourself, you won't want to feed your mind anything else.

We are at a point in history when, in my opinion, there's not much new to create—only ways to improve current products. So it's not a matter of coming up with a new recipe; it's more about adding your own spin to one that is already working. Headphones were invented in 1958 by John Koss, a Milwaukee-based jazz musician. Yes, they have been around awhile. Since then, obviously a lot has changed: today's headphones have better sound; can be smaller; and can have noise cancellation, a microphone, or Bluetooth technology. In my view, there is not much more room for improvement there. But somewhere on earth, one or more people had the vision to shake things up. They chose the right name and colors. There was one man who could make it all work perfectly: we now have Beats by Dre, and it owns the headphone market. What sets Beats so far apart from the competition? The headphones are not the greatest in the world, perhaps, but the company markets its products in a way I've never seen before. From Dr. Dre's and countless athletes' association with the brand, Beats has been able to dominate the market with only average products.

The GoPro is another product that amazes me. It's a video camera. But again, someone had the vision to revolutionize the camera world with an adventurous angle, and now the founder is a billionaire. Did he invent a new product? No. And where did all his money come from? Wealth is like the ocean. Remember, there is enough for all of us. We just have to figure out how to get a piece.

How can you change a really old business? Well, someone asked that question about the taxi world, and today we have Uber. Most of my peers use it. It's faster, cheaper, and a lot more convenient than a regular cab service. Is Uber a new idea? No. It is an old, working recipe but with a new twist, and millions of people are now using it. Again, if you desire to be rich, simply learn how to reach millions of people.

Waiting to become the perfect person to start pursuing your goals or to have the perfect product before you start selling is a recipe for disaster. Who you are and what you have today are enough to get you started. Perfection in anything is impossible to achieve anyway. Even the great Michael Jordan in his prime had flaws in his game. Daily improvement in you and your brand is how you go from novice to expert. Be the best you today, but work on being an even better you tomorrow.

The three products I've mentioned are only a few of countless examples of how people used their minds to achieve financial success. Right now, at this moment, someone somewhere is working on making one of the products around you better and will probably become a millionaire because of it. Look back ten years. How did cell phones, cars, TV, or movies look? Yes—completely different from how they look today. Opportunities are all around us. In ten years, few things will be the same as they are today.

What are you aiming for? To be a spectator or a creator? It is very easy to spectate and enjoy what others create (or, shall I say, improve). Remember all those people who wait in line for the iPhone. How many are there compared to the number that study the iPhone, come up with ideas to improve it, and knock on Apple's door until their ideas become part of the revolution? If owning an iPhone is worth waiting in line for, then imagine what contributing to the creation of the iPhone feels like. It is ironic how people abuse the most valuable resource they possess. Most of us are extremely fortunate and blessed to receive the gift of twenty-four hours a day for many years, yet we barely do anything worth remembering. We humans tend not to value what's handed to us, especially if the supply seems endless. It takes a strong mind to realize that the life clock is always ticking and that each second we waste is a second that we could have used to make a difference—not only in ourselves, but in the world around us.

Today, someone did not receive the twenty-four-hour gift, and tomorrow, unfortunately, someone else will not. Most of us have no clue when our last breath will be, yet we abuse time like we're guaranteed life forever. Start holding yourself accountable. We have no room to talk about how we cannot trust other people with as many promises we have broken with ourselves.

For example, you purchased a TV from a store with a thirty-day return policy; the TV breaks on day twenty-eight. What do you do? We both know you will march down to that store and handle the matter. But let's say you start a thirty-day goal. By next week, you'll forget what that goal even was. Who is holding you accountable?

Do the math. Most of us hold everything and everyone accountable but ourselves. We are quick to point out how others let us down, yet we are blind to the fact that we let ourselves down more than anyone else ever has. You have a goal to wake up at 6:00 a.m., but you snooze until 6:15 a.m. Ladies and gents, you have officially started your day by sleeping time away that you will never get back—and by letting yourself down. Over time, those fifteen extra minutes add up to days of your life.

How many times have you told yourself you would accomplish a goal but quit halfway through (or, worse, did not start at all)? How many New Year's resolutions, diets, and promises to change bad habits have you broken? My list of those is endless because, like many others, I made the mistake of assuming that quitting is a one-and-done event. Everything that you do is similar to planting a seed. Some seeds are extremely small, but what happens when you constantly feed them? They grow into big trees that produce many other seeds. That one time you quit years ago may be the reason why you now break promises to yourself daily, or even worse, not make any promises at all. Remember that the small things that you do today, whether good or bad, eventually add up big-time over the upcoming years.

Forget seeing with the eyes and start focusing on using your mind. It costs nothing and takes little to no effort to just imagine. What seeds are you planting in your mind? And, most important, where are you getting your seeds from? The news? Your peers? School? Your parents? Or wherever? Treat your mind as soil and your goals and dreams as seeds. I take care of my soil daily by selecting what I feed my mind. My goals and dreams, my seeds, include becoming a best-selling author, a motivational speaker, and a self-made millionaire. How will countless hours watching TV, going to the club, or spending money on the newest phone or Jordan shoes help me grow my seeds? We both know the answer to that question.

I am not opposed to enjoying life in the now, but having your priorities in proper order is a must to achieve success in any area of life. Your eyes should be reading more than watching TV; your body needs to take more action that will get you closer to your goals and dreams than dancing at the clubs. You can either live life as it comes or create the life you dream of and are fully capable of achieving. A or B: your choice.

Although having a vision can be simple, life itself is not. Take a second and think about your excuses for why you can't pursue the life you dream of and do the things that will make you scream, "Thank God it's Monday!" Most of us are not where we are by choice, although by a certain age, your situation is the result of choices you have made. We face obstacles: they may be kids, the environment, a lack of education, no support system, and so on. We all have to face situations that challenge our faith in ourselves and even in humanity.

I want you to really spend some time thinking about what could possibly go wrong if you pursue your goals and dreams, and what is stopping you right now. After you answer that, make a promise to yourself that this is the last time you will breathe life into your obstacles, reasons, and excuses for why you cannot pursue the life you want to live. Plain and simple, it does us no good to focus on those areas. And focus is power. Describe the circumstances that you do not want to occur, drop your excuses for why you can't be-gin the journey to becoming your true self, and then stamp on them. They do not play a part in the recipe for the life you are aiming to achieve.

CHAPTER 4

GOALS

You can't hit a target you cannot see, and you cannot see a target you do not have.

—Zig Ziglar

I remember that when I was in the fifth grade, a group of high school students came to my class to spread some knowledge. One thing they talked about was their goals. For whatever reason, out of everything they shared with us, that part spoke to me the most. The high school students shared how studies show that people with goals achieve more than people without them. A study was conducted by Harvard University, and between the students with goals and those without. The difference was astounding. The few students who had set goals for themselves financially outperformed in later years those who did not, by a large margin.

I remember saying to myself that if I didn't start learning about setting goals, one day I would remember that story and regret it. That day did come. I think about that moment in the fifth grade too often. Instead of setting goals, I made excuses for myself, such as, "I don't know how. I am too young. I am not smart enough. I have nothing to reach for," and so on. That was back in 1999 or 2000. Imagine if I had been courageous enough to start setting goals then. I would be an expert today, about fifteen years later. We do not think past a few days, a week, or a month when it comes to accomplishing tasks. We only do the things that deliver immediate results. After all, why work for years with no reward when you can work for a week and be comfortable? If I hadn't read *Think and Grow Rich* by Napoleon Hill, I would probably not understand the concept of working for nothing up front. But my fifth-grade moment is in the past, and none of us have the power to change that. What we can do is work on the now and future.

Goals are your target. If you don't clearly define them, you will have a hard time hitting them. Worse, if you don't have any, you will never hit one. What goals do you have for your finances, career, relationship, personal life, or spiritual life? If you don't have any goals, make it your goal to learn about the importance of goal setting this instant. I did not wake up one day and magically become a published author. It started with a vision to reach and inspire as many people as possible, and that vision turned into the idea of writing an inspirational book, and that idea turned into a goal that I focused on until it became a reality.

Goals are beyond powerful. Daily goals, weekly goals, monthly, yearly—the more goals you set and accomplish, the more fulfilling your life will be. Try it. Make it a goal tomorrow to accomplish ten tasks, big or small. At the end of the day, you will feel proud and accomplished and more confident in yourself than ever before. If you have never tried goal setting, start small. Remember that when you are learning a new skill, see yourself as a baby learning how to crawl. Once you learn how to crawl, you stand up, and from there you walk. The next thing you know, you're running around the house with more energy than a superhero. But never forget that those you see running the show started out crawling on their hands and knees.

As an adult, though, you'll find that people and life in general are not as kind as they were when you were a baby. That is why your "whys"the reasons you started and your end destination need to be in front of your face at all times. Your whys sometimes are the only push or pull you'll have to keep you going. Make your whys your best friends, the strength and the light you need when times get hard and dark. You will find out quickly that most of your journey consists of you and your whys versus all your fears, doubts, and insecurities, as well as unexpected events, people rejecting you, the ones you love not supporting you, and more. When you are at the bottom, learning how to crawl up to your goals and dreams, consider yourself lucky if you have one or two people supporting you. Do not worry, though. Once you reach the top, you will have plenty of love and support. You will have people screaming that they always knew you would make it and how much they always believed in you. Your only duty at that point will be to smile and say thank-you.

Goal setting is easier said than done. Trust me, I know. I have been battling with setting goals for years now, but it works. And the more goals you set and accomplish, the bigger your future goals will become. Never in a million years did I think I would write a book. I used to hate reading. As a matter of fact, my goal was to read as little as possible. But somehow, accomplishing that goal came so naturally, even though I did not know much about goal setting. You see how that works? When it is bad for you, it is just too easy to do. Whether you realize it or not, you are a master goal setter. It's only a matter of realizing what type of goals you are setting for yourself. Life, time, and the universe do not care what seed you plant. They will grow it for you.

In the past, my goals were to watch TV, go out and spend money, hang out with friends on the weekends, buy the most expensive of whatever I could afford (thinking things were making me a more valuable person), and make sure I at least got my annual raise. Whether I knowingly set those goals or they got done automatically is irrelevant. Again, life does not care. It will accept whatever you put into it, and it will indeed bless you with results accordingly. Automatic goals require no effort from you. They are as easy as breathing, but they will keep from ever reaching your full potential.

What results will you achieve from such goals in five, ten, or twenty years? Now you might be thinking that only kids play video games, watch a lot of TV, and go out. Well, you would be wrong. And even if you modified those goals, they would still fall along the same lines, such as watching more football and getting drunk with friends at home instead of doing it at the club. Plain and simple, the pattern just continues unless you change. My goals today are extremely different from my goals of the past; not because I got older, but because I grew up mentally and realized that the universe is at my fingertips.

I used to assume that because I was growing bigger physically that I was growing mentally, spiritually, and emotionally too. I fully believed that I was maturing in all aspects of life as I aged. Well, I was wrong, and I am sure that I am not alone in this. Your body grows with time, and for part of your life, so does the spiritual, emotional, and mental side. But there comes a point where developing those three aspects in a healthy way requires initiative from you. I use the word "healthy" because growth happens, whether in a negative or positive way. There will be a point in your life when your parents, friends, or teachers will not be able to help you grow mentally. If you are religious (which I highly encourage), there will be a point where your current pastor will not be able to help you grow spiritually. There will be a point when commitment, effort, and the person you prefer to date cannot help you grow emotionally.

If you do not seek self-improvement in the spiritual, mental, and emotional aspects of your life, then the day will come when you will hit a plateau. Goal setting for these aspects of your life is crucial. In the past, my main goal was to get my body strong so I could conquer any challenge in life. I figured that if I was strong physically, then I would be able to win most battles. Well, think about it—how many physical fights do you face daily, weekly, monthly, or even yearly? Most likely not many. But I guarantee that every day of your life since you have been able to understand the world around you, you have faced emotional, spiritual, and mental battles. For example, if you set an alarm for 5:00 a.m. and you hit the snooze button when that time comes, then you just lost a mental battle. If someone cuts you off as you're driving to work and you tell that person a thing or two, you just lost an emotional battle. If someone does you wrong and you hold a grudge instead of forgiving, according to the Bible, at least, you just lost a spiritual battle.

In my personal experience, maturing mentally has proved to be the most rewarding of all these aspects. The more I grow my mind, the more I seek to grow everything else. It seems like the more I expand my mind, the more I am able to accomplish physically. For example, I aim to lift more at the gym now. I crushed my first fitness competition because of how much I believed in myself. The better my heart started to feel and understand, the more I believed in and sought to understand a higher power. I am strictly speaking from my own experience. For you, it might be a different aspect that's the most important, but if what you choose to focus on most is physical, then I urge you to reconsider. Keep in mind that you will rarely face physical fights in this lifetime, even if you are a professional fighter. Your biggest battle will live in your mind.

We must also mature mentally, which is another reason that I say that your eyes will make you blind. Your parents, school peers, and random experiences can only teach you so much, and once those limits are reached, then you are no longer growing mentally.

The information and the knowledge required to change your situation will not appear before your two eyes. It needs to be a seed planted in your mind, and that seed has the power to give your eyes the vision they did not have before.

The universe and everything in it are yours for the taking, but you must aim for whatever it is you desire. The road is not an easy one, but judging by the people who are living life like a vacation, it is extremely rewarding. There is no such thing as a shortage. There is enough for all of us to share, and there will be enough for our children to share. But if you are only looking with your eyes, then you will see so little, and seeing so little plays with your mind and your emotions. You will not aim to make a million dollars a year because, in your eyes, it is not possible. After all, most people around you are aiming for average, safe, comfortable salaries, so why be different? Instead of aiming for freedom, you aim to be comfortable—for the simple fact that it is all your eyes can see.

It is extremely possible to aim for a million dollars a year. Just Google it. People all around the world are doing it year after year, so why not you? What makes them more special than you? Why did God choose them and not you? Why, why, why? Because you do not possess the knowledge and are not mentally mature enough to aim for a million dollars per year. Let me ask you this: if you could earn a million dollars a year doing something you absolutely hate, would you? Now imagine making the same money doing something you love. A lot of people on this planet do not have to imagine that. They are living it. And, no, they are not any more special than you and I. Just because others may be more book smart, better actors, more athletic, better singers, or whatever else, it doesn't mean they are more special than you. We're all created equally special. But it's up to you to produce special results.

How much you make is not truly the amount you want, wish for, or desire, it is the amount you yourself have settled for. I have a goal of earning a hundred thousand dollars a month in five years.

Scary, I know—that is more than a lot of people make in a year. But I took myself out of the "a lot of people" crowd a long time ago, so to me, that goal is extremely achievable. It will not be easy, but it is simple. Wake up every day and do whatever is necessary to reach that goal. Have my whys in front of me daily, and always remember that every second counts. Quitting and/or settling for less will not get me any closer to accomplishing that goal.

While that goal is scary, it is still simply a mind-set. Someone is reading this book now and laughing at that because they probably make that in a week, if not less. Bill Gates makes that amount in how much time? He is not an alien, ladies and gents. He is a human just like you and me. If it is possible for one, then it is possible for two.

In setting your goals, keeping things simple is your best option. My financial goal is not to have or create a million-dollar idea. It is to create something that will reach millions. If you have a product or service that serves millions, no matter how much profit you make, you will be able to kiss your financial struggles good-bye. One of my personal goals is to inspire people, to remind them of how powerful they are and that they should always have faith. The biggest "check" I aim for is for one person to come up to me and express how much my teaching has changed his or her life. I can aim for a million dollars, but it will never equal knowing that I changed a life. For that is priceless.

TV, social media, magazines, and even your surroundings have the potential to be your worst enemies when it comes to goal setting. It seems like those outlets glorify people with "natural" talent. *Fox NFL Sunday* is all about the players on the field and the coaches. You rarely hear about the hundreds of others behind the scenes who make those games possible. Again, your eyes will blind you. Who do you see on TV or on the big screen at the theater? The actors and the big stars, as if they actually made the movie instead of simply playing parts. They fail to show all the other characters behind the scenes who contributed to making that motion picture happen, and that plays tricks on our minds. If I am not good at acting, then how can I ever be in movies? Keep in mind that more people behind the scenes made that motion picture possible than the few you see on the screen.

In school, who got the most attention from other students and teachers? Probably the star athletes instead of the students with good grades. Funny how that works. Now think about the richest people in the world and pick out how many of them are athletes, movie stars, or entertainers. What you see is not always the truth. Just because someone is glorified does not mean he or she is more special than you and me. It does not mean that such people can live their goals and dreams while you and I, who were not blessed in the same manner, are only capable of working for a boss until social security kicks in. The talent and skills of these people look like they came with instant fortune and fame, but even their stories are deeper than that.

If you know history, you know that instant fame can be your worst enemy. The question is, what do you bring to the table? It does not matter whether your talent and skills get recognized publicly by millions of others; they only need to influence them. Stop looking at what is being displayed in front of you, for the simple fact is that there is so much more to life than the eyes can see. Focus. Focus on what you have to offer, not what you do not. Forget about everything that you don't have or that you are not capable of producing. Focus on what is possible for you, and dedicate your life to achieving that goal. We all have the potential to play in the NFL—a few of us on the field, but a lot of us behind the scenes.

CHAPTER 5

THE BIG PICTURE

The big picture doesn't just come from distance; it also comes from time.

—*Simon Sinek*

What exactly is the big picture? To me, "the big picture" means that one goal you envision every time you think about which dream come true would give your life the ultimate meaning. My big picture is to be the next Anthony Robbins—which is actually a scary thing for me to write. I still do not understand how Robbins does the things he does because he is unbelievable, and mentally I am not there yet. Robbins did not wake up one day and turn into who he is today. It took him countless years, and I am pretty sure that at one point, he was where you and I may be today—which is at the crawling stage. I would be a fool to think that I could go on stage today and perform as well as him, but that does not mean I cannot be there ten or fifteen years from now if I follow his path. Robbins's recipe for his massive success is not a secret. He has offered countless seminars and book and audio programs that I can study and learn from. Better yet, what if he took me under his wing? As unlikely as that is, it is not impossible. If it takes me twenty-plus years to produce similar results to Robbins's, then so be it. When you truly have your life goal in place, then how much time it takes you to get there becomes irrelevant. As long as you are breathing, your only option is to breathe life into that goal.

To be the next Anthony Robbins, in my opinion, is as hard as being the next Michael Jordan. Many have tried, but all have failed thus far. Why not me? Why can't I be the one to reach that level? I have asked myself empowering questions daily about my big picture, and somehow I usually find the answers. Asking yourself empowered questions is one of the key elements you need to get your mind thinking about possibilities that are not within your reach, that your eyes are not capable of seeing, and that very few, if any, of the people you know of are reaching. I am a motivational speaker, and my current big picture is to rise to a level where I am invited to deliver speeches to Harvard graduates and the president of the United States. As of right now, I speak to youth, but as I have mentioned, I already have my big target in mind. Every day I do something that gets me closer to hitting that target. Remember that a journey of a thousand miles begins with a single step.

Why is it crucial to have a big picture in mind? For me, at least, it keeps me on my toes; it keeps me learning constantly. It pushes me to grow better and stronger—mentally, emotionally, and spiritually. As knowledgeable as I am today, what I know is by far not good enough for me to stand in front of a Harvard crowd or the president and deliver the type of quality message necessary for that caliber of audience. If I got an opportunity today to speak at Harvard, would I take it? Of course—for the simple fact that anyone can bring something to the table, even that homeless guy you pass by every day. He could easily share his story and inspire you to make better decisions. My goal is not simply to talk at Harvard once and be done. It goes a lot deeper than that. My goal is to have a relationship with Harvard, so that every year, someone like me, who currently holds only a high school diploma, partners up with one of the top schools in the United States to better educate its students.

If you think I'm crazy, that is fine. You are supposed to. People are supposed to look at your dreams and goals and laugh at you, doubt you, and tell you, "Good luck!" That's how you know you are on the right path of living among the top 10 percent. If the majority agrees with your goals and big picture, then you are aiming way too low—which a lot of people tend to do, including me, for years. I was very successful, but I was successful at mediocre goals. The first step is to grow your mind. Once your knowledge increases, your vision expands, your targets are higher and more challenging, and you begin to develop the courage to face your fears head on and learn how to get back up when life knocks you down.

Grow your mind, grow your life. It is really that simple. People ask me all the time to train them at the gym. A few years ago, I wanted to be a personal trainer, but I was also working on my mind daily during that time. The more my mind grew, the more I realized that, at least for me, that target was too low. If I help you train at the gym, and as a result, you are now in the best shape of your life, will your life be any different? Yes, but in limited ways. And who knows—the fat person inside you might defeat you again once I am gone. Now if I train your mind, and as a result, you become mentally stronger, then there is no limit to what you can accomplish, including becoming more physically fit. Training your body will help you physically for the most part, but training your mind has the potential to change your life in unimaginable ways. That is why today, I have devoted my time to helping people to grow their minds instead of their bodies. It is harder to train the mind, yes, but it is by far more rewarding for that individual and for myself.

No amount of money will ever be more valuable to me than people expressing how I changed their lives.

I have come to learn and truly understand how everything you do and fail to do add up to your life. The seconds of your life add up to the minutes of your life, the minutes to the hours, the hours to the days, the days to the weeks, the weeks to the months, the months to the years, and the years into who you are today. Every second truly matters, and it is crucial to be as productive as possible every single day of your life. Your big-picture target is there to keep you on track. It creates smaller targets that you will need to hit in order to mentally mature enough to take aim at that major goal. Imagine your big picture, though, as a goal that is constantly giving birth to an even bigger goal. My big picture today may not be the same a few years from now. Who knows—I may want to exceed Tony Robbins one day.

To create your life and where you'd like to be in the far future, you must begin by creating your day as much as possible, this instant. You may not be able to control your work or school schedule, but you may be able to control the time you get out of bed every day, which is a crucial step that very few follow. People complain about not having enough time, but they never take the time to learn how to manage time. Managing time is a simple process. Plan your days, weeks, and months ahead as much as possible. If you are new to this, start with planning your next day ahead of time. Create a schedule and dictate the areas you have complete control over.

If you have to work at 9:00 a.m., for example, you are able in most cases to get up at 5:00 a.m., be productive for yourself first, and then go to work. If you have a decent lunch break, manage that by bringing your own food and eating for half the time and reading for the other half. Remember that every second counts, including the ones you spend looking for the closest parking spot. It will not do you any good to complain about time. The universe will not bless you with an extra hour. It is up to you to learn and under-stand how to maximize your daily twenty-four hours. Kevin Hart, who is someone whose accomplishments I admire, does this more effectively than anyone else I am aware of. Hart somehow makes movies and TV shows, performs stand-up comedy, and makes TV appearances and still has time to spend with family and enjoy life.

If you are thinking it is easy, then why aren't other people in his industry doing the same things? Hart makes it look easy. Although I do not know him personally, it is obvious to see that he is where he is today because he by far outhustles everyone else. Hart seems to have his goals and big picture in mind and is laser focused on achieving every single one of them. His big picture has given birth to so many other bigger pictures over the years that I could write a whole book on that subject alone. Hart is not the funniest person on the planet—hell, I think I am funnier than him. He is not the best actor, not the best-looking guy, and definitely not the tallest guy around. But he keeps it plain and simple. He allows no soul on the planet to outwork him. As short as he is, he has the power to look down on millions of people if he chooses to. There is no limit to how big you can dream. Learn how to be the universe, for you are full of endless potential.

CHAPTER 6

DAILY COMMITMENT

K eep saying that today does not matter. You will go to sleep,
wake up, and find out you've been saying the same thing for
five years now. Make every second count.

One day, you woke up and decided that it was time to get yourself in the best shape of your life. You visited your local gym and
talked to a trainer, pouring out your dreams and goals, and walked
out with a membership and a fitness plan that has been proven
to work. The next day, you woke up at 5:00 a.m. and made it to
the gym at 6:00 a.m. You were able to maintain your motivation
through the end of the week. The next week came around, and
your body was still hurting from the previous week, your energy
and motivation to continue were down, and the voices in your
head were reciting a list of reasons why an extra thirty minutes of
sleep won't hurt.

You already know how this story ends. You remember paying
for a gym membership that you haven't used in months.

This example can be spun in millions of ways, but the point
behind it is simple. If you develop a habit of breaking your word to
yourself, over time that habit will only grow if you do not address
and correct it from the beginning. In my opinion and experience,

daily commitment is the hardest step to master. Even today as I write this book, I still have an issue with daily commitment. It is a weakness I recognize, and I have been working on getting better. We have been practicing not keeping our word to ourselves ever since we can remember. Worse, the people around us do not keep their word, and technology helps us in not keeping our word. The snooze button allows us more time to avoid reality. It allows you to believe that you have all the time in the world and that five extra minutes of sleep won't hurt. Today it is five extra minutes. Next month, it will be fifteen, and come five years, how much time will you have wasted?

Is this the fault of technology or the environment you grew up in? What excuses can you come up with for not being able to keep your word to yourself? I could come up with a mile-long list, but it would only build a mile-long wall between myself and my goals and dreams. No excuses are acceptable when you aim to accomplish extraordinary results in life. Every time you point a finger at the outside world for why you can't, you are slipping further into mediocrity. Every second that you spend asleep is a second that someone else spends working. There is no magic to living a successful life. Keep it simple and outwork the other guy every single day.

It is easy to wake up at 4:00 a.m. "every day" for two days, but what about that third day when your body is screaming no, when the excuses in your head are coming down like a hurricane, when that voice is in there saying that one more hour will not make a difference, go ahead and hit the snooze button? We have all had similar experiences. It is amazing how easy it is for the negative voices to come out and take control, telling you it is OK that today will not make a difference, selling you on every excuse possible to make you buy into how just this one time won't hurt. That is why a strong mind-set is your number one weapon to be successful in life. From the second that alarm goes off, the battle in the mind begins. If your whys for getting up are not clear, if you are not passionate about your daily work, if your mind-set is not trained to defeat those demons within, then nine times out of ten, you will lose the battle.

Maybe that voice is right; this one time may not hurt—but it sure does not help or promote the habit of holding yourself accountable. No matter how you are feeling, the best thing you can do is stick to the plan. Eric Thomas said it best: "At the end of your feelings is nothing, but at the end of every principle is a promise." When you make decisions based on emotions, your actions are inconsistent since your feelings may change based on current situation. Your feelings change constantly. Numerous situations have the power to change and shape how you feel at any given time. If you operate primarily on your feelings, it is next to impossible to stay consistent. No one wakes up and feels the exact same way every single day, but you do have the choice to follow the exact same principles daily. Learn how to stay committed to principles instead, because regardless of how you feel, they will remain the same.

Let's put principles into play. First of all, there is no such thing as a new principle. They have all been around ever since humans started walking the earth. The Bible is loaded with principles. The only thing that has changed about its principles is the wording. (I am not telling you to learn about the Bible, but remember that it is the best-selling book of all time. Something must be special about it. Five billion copies sold cannot be a fluke.) Why is it important to primarily act based on principles? Principles never change, regardless of feelings or circumstances. Principles force you to hold yourself accountable, which many of us rarely, if ever, do. The Personal Excellence principles web page (http://personalexcellence.co/blog/life-principles/) is a great resource for more than one hundred principles. How many of them do you currently follow? How many, if you added them to your life today, would have an instant effect? How many did you not even know existed?

Mastering anything in this life requires knowledge, practice, and action, but as I've said, the initiative for learning must first come from you. Learning how to stay committed daily will take time and work, especially if you are older and have been living life as it comes. But it's never too late. The best thing you can do is to fall in love with knowledge. The day you stop learning should be the same day you stop breathing. Bill Gates, to this day, still learns. The number-one step is to look in the mirror and promise yourself that you will start holding yourself accountable and that you will take steps and actions each and every day to learn how to master the art of commitment. From there on, ladies and gents, it becomes simple (but still not easy). You have your heading. Now all you have to do is gain the necessary knowledge to navigate your ship in that direction.

Why is daily commitment so crucial? Well, why not? When you waste today, you most likely will be blessed to breathe again tomorrow. So why does one day matter so much? That attitude will take you into one, two, or five years of saying, "Well, it is only one day. It does not matter." Every day matters. Remember that you may get another Monday or Tuesday, but you will never get that actual date back. Monday has a fresh, new date every week; it is not recycled from the previous week. So stop focusing on the day and start seeing the date that you will never see again and make it count.

What would you like to accomplish? For me, right now, I am working on being a motivational speaker, and by the time this book is published, I will already be speaking. Notice how I wrote this sentence and the confidence that it showcases. These are the types of words you have to express to yourself and others. There is no such thing as a maybe. Either you will get it done, or you will not go to sleep until you do. Again, commitment and holding yourself accountable to that is crucial. Back to the current goal of being a motivational speaker: my daily commitment includes waking up at 4:50 a.m. daily. (I am working on making it 3:50 a.m.) Before I do anything other than the essentials, like brushing my teeth, I meditate for an hour to ease my mind and give thanks for another twenty-four hours. After that hour, I eat breakfast while listening to a positive message, usually a Les Brown speech. Then I envision myself speaking in front of a select audience that includes sport teams, colleges, Harvard students, the young, the old, and on TV, and my ultimate goal of being on stage, speaking in front of eighty thousand people. Once my mind, heart, and soul connect, my mouth opens and I begin to speak—no script, no preparation— and the words just flow like a river.

Today, I feel as if I can conquer the world and any challenge that it presents, which is a great way to feel. But let's be honest, as of right now, there are still things that I cannot yet conquer. But I am not afraid to fail. If you are afraid to fail (or, should I say, learn), how will not trying help you conquer that fear—or any other fear, for that matter? One of the best questions you can ask yourself when you are facing a challenge is, "If I do this but don't get the results I want, will that kill me?" When the answer is no, then go for it. I will probably be terrified the day I have to stand in front of thousands to deliver a speech, but even if I deliver the worst speech in history, will it kill me? Of course not. Obviously, I hope to do great, but regardless of the outcome, I will have gained new experience and knowledge that will have me standing one step closer to my ultimate life goal. Failure is still learning. People judging you by those failures is a sign that you are trying, and you need to keep trying until you produce your desired results. Remember that the clock stops for no one, so regardless of the many failures, challenges, ups and downs, rejections, fears, and self-doubts, keep moving with the clock.

Who I am today will be good enough for my future goals and dreams. Again, daily improvement is crucial. Your greatness today has the potential to be even greater tomorrow. Do not neglect daily improvements, for you will eventually fall back in line with the average, or worse. Imagine the United States fighting with the same weapons today as it did in the world wars. Imagine a company making the same type of cell phones it was making ten years ago. Imagine that you finished high school or college five years ago and never sought further education of any sort. That is the story for many people, including me at one point. We assumed that with age came wisdom. We assumed that there was no difference between being alive and living life. I know a lot of people who are much older than I, yet they do not possess half the knowledge. I am not any better and definitely not smarter than those people. The difference is my commitment to daily learning. You can afford to miss a meal, but you cannot afford to miss out on knowledge.

CHAPTER 7

FAITH

*None of us knows what might happen even the next min-
ute, yet still we go forward. Because we trust. Because we
have Faith.*

—Paulo Coelho, *Brida*

While I was at work one day, I got a message to return a
customer's call, so I did. The voice on the other end was
that of a man whom I had never met before. He told me he would
be coming in soon to see me for assistance. When he came in,
he asked for me. He was an older, white male wearing a color-
ful T-shirt and a long skirt (for lack of a better term). I assisted
him, and he was very pleased with my service. He continued asking about my life and how I was spending it. After a few minutes
of talking, he made sure I kept his number, gave me his website
address, and told me to call him again.

Later that week, I did just that. I visited his website and saw
that this man happened to be a successful businessman. But more

important, he had been studying the Hare Krishna movement, a branch of Hinduism, for more than forty years. Since then, he has become a mentor of mine. The way he speaks, plus his energy, passion, and knowledge, is unlike anything I have ever been around before. It is nearly impossible to be around this man and not feel at peace. And his house is one of a kind like a two-story tree house made for adults. You can see for yourself on his website (http://halekrishna.com/). Out of everything I have learned from him, these two things spoke to me the most. He told me that I am not black. Imagine an old, bald-headed white man having the nerve to tell me I'm not black. How dare he? I had been looking in the mirror for twenty-seven years and seeing a black man, and a very proud one at that. I did not interrupt. I chose to listen instead, and that was the best thing I could have done at that moment.

He explained to me how I am much more than my body, my skin, or my gender. He took me beyond the physical and got me seeing myself as an infinite being in a human body. Since then, physically I am still the same size, but mentally I feel like I'm much more mature because of that realization. The second thing that struck me most was the concept of quality. He spoke of the importance of spending time on quality. I have heard the word "quality" all my life, as I am sure you have also. But he described quality like I have never heard it described before. He was 100 percent right. He explained how everything that he does is with his faith, resulting in the highest-quality performance. He made me realize why I like coming to talk to him. The quality I feel around this man is unlike anything I have ever felt, and because of it, my mind, my soul, and my body have improved dramatically.

Why is that story worth mentioning? You attract what you seek. By that time, I had already been looking beyond what I saw with my two eyes. I was already using my mind and was seeking higher understanding and enlightenment. The student was ready, and sure enough, one of the best teachers showed up. This mentor of mine told me that the reason he kept in contact with me was because he could feel my energy; he could see the light in me. So what you seek will find you. Always have faith.

I spent the first twenty-five years of my life focusing on all the physical aspects. After high school I went to college, but I eventually stopped because I was going through a divorce. Back then, I did not have the knowledge or mind-set to realize that my education and personal life had nothing to do with each other. Instead, I created every excuse to quit. My spiritual and mental sides were as out of date as a landline compared to the newest iPhone. One of my biggest mistakes (which a lot of people make) was assuming that mental and spiritual growth are automatic.

I did achieve success during the time when I simply focused on the physical side of things—or so I thought. With my divorce, everything in my world came crashing down, and I ended up spending just about two years living an inch away from suicide daily. What I experienced during those times seemed impossible to overcome, but it revealed to me how weak I was. Yes, physically, I was built and strong, but divorce is not a physical battle. Having someone whom you loved for years stop loving you is something that you have to be emotionally strong for. I was like a ship without an anchor, a quality crew, or a captain. The moment the storm hit me, I was doomed. I had no faith and no hope for the future. I could not see beyond what was happening at the current moment. I felt like life was over, and even worse, I was too proud to ask for help, especially since I was a leader in the marines. I felt that the men would look down on me and see me as a failure. Instead, I put on a mask and went to work looking like Superman every day. Meanwhile, inside I was a crying, little child.

Why is faith important? Faith is necessary for all areas of life, whether personal or professional. We all have a certain level of faith. When you fly, you literally put your faith in the airplane itself and the pilot to take you off the ground and land you across the country or across the globe. As valid an example as that is, in my opinion it's weak. You and millions of other people have faith in airplanes and pilots because people fly daily, and the act of flying has been around for quite some time now. We have faith that a physically healthy baby will be able to walk one day, so we encourage that baby even when he or she keeps falling down. That act has been performed billions of times, so that type of faith is automatic at this point.

Let's talk about the faith that you need when times get hard, when there is no light in sight, when nobody believes in you, when everything that could go wrong has gone wrong, and when you get buried deep in the ground. Let's talk about the faith that is required to overcome such a time. That level of faith, ladies and gents, demands believing in yourself the way no words can express. More important, it demands that you believe in your creator. After all, your mother's womb was simply your first house, not your initial birthplace. Whatever you choose to call your creator is between you and you. The valuable point here is to understand that you come from a higher place than this earth.

Faith is what drives you forward in times of uncertainty. Many great things on this earth exist today because of faith. Take the Wright brothers, for example. I can only imagine how much faith it took for them to fly that first airplane. Think about it. Everything you do on a daily basis is actually done with faith. You have faith in the food products that you eat, the medicines from your doctor, that your car brakes will work, and that the school system will properly educate your child. The list goes on. Whether you know it or not, you have been living life by faith. So what is missing at this point? For me personally, it was faith in myself and a higher consciousness; knowing that I can achieve anything I put my mind to. Still, to this day, my faith is one of the aspects I am still working on. I see Tony Robbins on stage and say to myself, "I can never be as good as him." And thus far, I have proven myself right.

Life is a constant battle. Our faith is something we must continually work on to get beyond where we currently are. It took a lot of faith for me to write this book, but it will take a lot more to publish it and make it part of my success story. A lot of us are waiting until we know all the answers before we take action, and that only leads to procrastination. You will never have all the answers or know all the dos and don'ts ahead of time. Constant action is a must to even keep you in the game of life. Constant action equals constant learning and improvement. If you truly want to learn and improve, then be part of the lessons instead of hiding behind books, seminars, and things like that. Do you need to read books and go to seminars? Of course you do. But let's say you want to learn how to swim. Reading about swimming and doing all the research in the world will not do you any good until you get in the water and experience it for yourself.

I have been in sales for many years now, and I am still amazed at the number of potential clients who still use the line, "I need to do more research," regardless of how much information they already have. For example, at GNC, customers come in all the time talking about their dream bodies and fitness goals. Once we link their goals to the supplements they may need, all of a sudden, they want to go home and do further research. Walking into a GNC and asking questions *is* researching your fitness goals. Then, if needed, Google for five minutes and verify. Beyond that, people are showing a lack of commitment to their own word. A lot of people like to talk about what they want to accomplish, but very few are willing to take action. Buying supplements for my body is one of my easiest decisions.

I could be wrong, but in this lifetime, I will be blessed with only one body. Spending a few hundred dollars to stay as healthy as possible is a no-brainer. The people who walk out of GNC to do more "research"—it's really about the cost—are the same people who smoke and drink and buy the latest phone, purse, and shoes without thinking twice. But, yup, when it comes to the only body they will ever have, their money is tight. We spend hours watching TV, playing games, and going out on a regular basis like it is second nature to us. But why aren't more people focused on improving and creating better lives for themselves? A lack of faith is one reason. A lack of faith will keep that idea buried in your head. A lack of faith will stop you from writing the next best-selling novel. It will keep you in a job you dislike or an abusive relationship. A lack of faith will mentally cripple you—and even physically, to a certain extent.

All roads in life have one final destination, and that's death. A day wasted is a day closer to your grave. Why live a safe and small life? I believe that we tend to forget that life will eventually end. We waste time like there's an endless supply of it. We bury ourselves in what-ifs before we even try anything: "What if this happens? People will look at me differently. And what if I mess up? People will laugh at me." But what if you succeed? How will your life change? The most valuable advice I can give you on what-ifs is, if it's not going to kill you and/or harm or violate the rights of anyone else, then go for it.

This takes us into "someday." Someday is the busiest day of the week—have you noticed that? Someday I will quit my job and start my own business. Someday I'll lose weight, write a song, and buy my dream car and house. What's on your schedule for someday? I went from having a goal to publish this book by a specific date to "someday." It wasn't until I slapped myself and got out of someday that I went back to pursuing my goal. Someday does not exist. Yet we plan for that day more than any other. Someday is only a prison for your thoughts, ideas, dreams, and goals. See tomorrow's future, but have the faith to start acting on it today without knowing all the details. Successful people are those who can predict the future a little but have faith to take immediate action.

CHAPTER 8
YOUR CIRCLE

*Know yourself; keep your circle tight. Keep your friends
and your work circle tight.*

—*Rita Ora*

W hy an entire chapter on "your circle"? And what do I even
mean by that? Your circle is the set of people you spend
most of your time with—most importantly, your free time. I understand that you cannot pick who your parents are or even whom
you go to school with or work with. But what you do have complete
control over is whom you spend your free time with and the things
that you do together. When we look at people who have accomplished goals that seem unreachable to most, we find that they had
like-minded friends. Their circles contained people who were also
aiming high in life—big dreamers. Mark Zuckerberg, the founder of Facebook, was building websites way before that. This guy
did not become a billionaire by luck or mistake. At a young age,
Zuckerberg had a vision of building a platform that would easily

connect the world together. He accomplished that by surrounding himself with like-minded people. Thanks to the brilliant team surrounding Zuckerberg, he literally owns the social media world today.

Take an inventory of your current circle and the activities you spend most of your free hours on. Who in your circle has billionaire dreams? Who works on self-improvement? Who aims to invent a new product or improve an existing one? Plain and simple, how many people in your circle even have written goals or even talk about them seriously? When you and your circle get together, what do you talk about? What do you spend time doing? Birds of a feather flock together. If you are spending time with people without visions for their future, chances are that you yourself have no vision. You are simply part of the circle's mediocre mix.

Getting to success and living a life of freedom is not an easy road. You will need to make sacrifices at times. It's hard to stay on the road, especially when you are just working based on hope and faith. Let's get personal and talk about parents. How many parents do you know who sit with their kids and preach that the power of the universe is within them and that they can accomplish anything they set their minds to? Did your parents ever tell you anything like that? In my own case, by far, no. My parents grew up with nothing, and they raised my siblings and me on next to nothing. We never heard any talk about dreams or goals, planning for the future, or achieving financial freedom. The only things my parents taught me were the things they knew were possible: finishing school and getting a decent-paying job. No one to this day has told me that whatever my mind can conceive, I can achieve; that I can be as successful as I want to be. I love my parents, but they were not an example to follow or to spend my free time with when I reached the age where I could move around. The environment I grew up in had no dreams or hopes, so I basically had none that stretched beyond what I saw with my eyes.

There are millions of people, if not billions, who were raised and are living in a similar environment. The one I grew up in was not the worst, but who is to blame now for a lack of wisdom and encouragement to be anything that you want to be? Information is everywhere and easily obtained today. A cell phone is almost like a mystical device, yet how many people do you know who use it to learn and improve themselves? YouTube is loaded with educational videos, and you can easily read books with a Kindle app on your phone just about anywhere. But how many people watch meaningless videos on YouTube instead of educational ones? How many people do you know who use the Kindle app more than the Facebook app? Success is not about being born lucky. It is about creating a strong system for your life. It is important to have goals, but it is even more crucial to build a system, a platform that you can plant your goals on.

The best thing that you can do is figure out who you want to be and start building a circle, a system based on your ultimate purpose in life. Whichever path you choose, trust and believe that someone else out there has done it before. The law of attraction is on your side—believe in it and use it. Imagine a fifteen-year-old who says, "I want to be the best real-estate investor in the world." He or she goes on YouTube and starts studying there, then to the local library to read books on the subject. After saving enough money to buy a real-estate investing game, he or she seeks out a real-estate investor to volunteer with for a few hours here and there. Do the math. If this kid continues on that path and keeps learning and improving, by the time he or she is twenty-five years old, where do you see this young person?

I did not mention doing anything that costs real money or that most of us, especially people living in the United States, cannot do. The road map was extremely simple. From fifteen to twenty-five is ten years of experience. Now imagine this kid now a man at thirty-five, forty-five, fifty-five years of age. If this kid does not accomplish the goal of becoming number one, he or she might at least be in the top ten of the field, and living among the stars is not a bad place to settle for. Now take that same kid but is fifteen and has no goals. He or she just goes to school, hangs with friends and plays video games, chases boys or girls in the clubs, goes to college, and gets a job. At twenty-five, where do you think he or she will be? Which version would you bet your money on to be financially successful? Being smart or naturally gifted, or being born in the right situation, only counts for so much. Success is designed for all of us free humans to achieve, from the smartest to the least smart. You can be successful. But you must take inventory of your thoughts, dreams, and goals related to your circle and what you spend your time doing.

I believe that a person should start using five-year plans at the age of ten and live the rest of life following five-year road maps. Enjoy being ten years old, do what kids do, but have a road map to where you want to be by the time you are fifteen. Yes, enjoy being fifteen, chase the girls or boys and play video games, but spend more time getting to know the world beyond where you live. Get to know the books that you don't find in a classroom. Learn about success that you probably will not find in your backyard, and have your road map for the age of twenty. I am sure by now that you get the point. Enjoy your current life, but spend time on building and preparing for the future. You will enjoy a higher quality of life over time. There is a major difference in quality between a Lamborghini and a Toyota. Both cars will take you from A to B, but which one would you rather have? Start building your life on high quality and make decisions based on what will result in the high-quality enjoyment. A lot of people can go to any old club and party, but imagine the quality of your time at your favorite club as the owner, or even as a multimillionaire.

As you build your five-year plan, having the right circle that fits your future is an important step. What's better—four dead batteries or one good one? What's better—four friends who are focused on video games, drinking, dancing, and getting the latest iPhone or two friends who are focused on self-improvement and accomplishing the billionaire dream? Again, do the math. Achieving success is pretty much a numbers game: are you adding or subtracting? Everything that you've done in the past results in who you currently are. If you spend five years of your life mostly doing things that do not add up to success, you can't be successful.

One of the most valuable skills I've developed is how to do life math. When I look back, I see why and how I was at that average place. I understand that I never aimed at any major goals. How I would love to go back to being fifteen but with a passion for being an author, a motivational speaker, and a successful multimillionaire entrepreneur. I would be at the beach house today, enjoying life my way while inspiring millions of people. But the past is the past. Even someone with billions cannot pay to turn back the hands of time. So today, my focus is on making the rest of my life the very best that it can possibly be.

Throughout my life, I have heard people saying, "Mind your own business." But, in my opinion, very few people know the actual meaning of the words. For me, it used to mean "stop being nosy"—or that I was not welcome right then. Today, though, it truly means that I should mind my own business—as in, take care of the business of my life: build my future, create profitable ideas, and grow myself. Pay close attention the next time you and your friends get together. What do you talk about? Most people just talk about other people and what they do. They discuss celebrity news, football games, who is sleeping with whom. Plain and simple, most people spend time talking about subjects that add nothing to their lives. While you are talking about what Kim and Kanye named their baby, they, on the other hand, are talking about how they can grow their net worth. While you are worrying about which celebrity is dating another, they are getting paid for public appearances.

Meanwhile, you are dreading Monday because that is when you go back to that job you dislike and that barely pays the rent.

While you are sitting at the bus stop counting your quarters and somehow got the newest phone, talking about how Floyd Mayweather can't read, the Money Man is sitting on more than half a billion dollars and living a lifestyle that isn't even possible in your dreams. Again, what do you and your peers talk about? Ideas, dreams, and goals? Or everything but?

Everything adds up. I do my math based on people who are where I would like to be. Bill Gates, in case you couldn't tell, is one of my biggest inspirations. I have a habit of asking myself, "What would Bill Gates do? What would he talk about? Who is in his circle?" And I seem to always get his guidance without him even knowing it. Have a system, and live your life in accordance. McDonald's, the most successful "small" business in the world, has one of the best systems ever. The company was not built with the goal of making the best burgers. Instead, it focused on having the best system through which to provide the best fast-food experience. The greatness of McDonald's speaks for itself. Millions of people can make better burgers than McDonald's, but no one has a better system for selling more burgers. Your life has to be a great system, and from that platform, everything else follows. Everything else will fall into place, from your goals, your dreams, your future plans, your circle, and the things you do with your free time.

Opinions are one thing that you are guaranteed to find an abundance of. Unfortunately, most opinions come from people without a track record of success. They are too afraid to take their own advice, or they give you advice based on their own failures (or accomplishments that do not add up to much). Remember that 80 percent of people are just getting by in life. They're all around you, and their advice is free. But it could potentially end up being extremely costly for you. Whose voices have you been listening to? I do believe that every human can learn from every other; in a way, all opinions are important. But how you process lessons and opinions is what matters most. At this point, I can squeeze positives from just about any words or situation. I can sit and have a conversation with a homeless man and learn something. I can learn about his childhood, teenage life, and the decisions he made all the way up to how his current life is going. It is possible to come out with a better understanding of my own life. Maybe I am doing some of the same things today that he did yesterday, or maybe I can gain enough understanding about his mistakes that can help me deliver a plan to our youth on how to avoid that path. I can almost guarantee that no one makes a goal to be homeless; yet today, thousands of people are without homes, and that number will be higher tomorrow.

Have you ever been too scared to discuss your goals and dreams with your friends or even parents because they might not understand? I have. I have been too scared to talk to my peers about my goals and dreams. And when I finally did, the responses were rather dull. It is hard for others to believe that something is possible for you that they have not achieved or don't believe is possible for themselves. For example, say you met Bill Gates and told him that you want to invent a product that will revolutionize the world and help you become a billionaire in the process. Then you tell the same thing to your neighbor, who is working hard and saving his money for retirement. Which one of the two do you believe will support your dream more? Which one do you believe will share words of wisdom and encouragement with you? The crazy thing about life is that anyone you listen to has the potential to be right. Whichever seed you believe is the truth is the one that has the best chance to grow.

Let's get closer to home and talk about those little voices in your head. Yes, we all have them. These voices are constantly feeding you thoughts, ideas, and opinions. Have you ever really sat back and evaluated what they say? Unknowingly, you have the power to be your own worst enemy. Whatever comes out of your mouth and whatever physical action you take was first processed within your mind. Your actions, reactions, emotions, and ideas are 100 percent your responsibility. The only way for the voices in your head to produce positive outcomes is to feed your mind positive food.

CHAPTER 9

WHERE IT ALL BEGINS: THE SECRET

We know what we are, but know not what we may be.

—William Shakespeare, "Hamlet"

In my opinion, the word "secret" is overused. Advertisers use it to get people interested in their products or services, and most of the time, the word in that context is deceiving. The human race has been around for thousands and thousands of years. Do you really believe that there are many secrets to life at this point? Do you actually believe that some fitness guru has a secret way to lose weight, that the business guru that preaches his secret to success has something new to teach? The only real secrets at this point are the ones the government hides from the public, but even those can sometimes be found with a little Internet research. There is no secret way to accomplish anything anymore. If you are dreaming about it, it has probably been done, and you can simply follow the blueprint.

On a personal level, I have been lifting weights and studying fitness ever since I was fifteen years young. I am now twenty-seven, and I have yet to learn a "secret" to fitness. There is only information that has been available for years that I have not yet discovered. Learning about fitness and achieving my fitness goals required the mentality of destroying my body at the gym, but more important, I had to learn to feed my mind with the knowledge that is available to us all. That's how you accomplish any goal in life.

The word "secret" is one I dislike due to the traps it places in your mind-set. For the longest time, I searched and searched for the secret to financial success, happiness, forgiveness, and love and acceptance. Since very few people are truly happy, successful, and living their dreams, it only made sense to me at the time that they must know something the rest of us do not. I went on a quest to find that secret, and if a book, article, blog, or video had the word "secret" attached to it, I researched it. Needless to say, I never found any secrets. I gained a lot of valuable knowledge and wisdom, and I learned a lot about my past mistakes, poor decisions, and mediocre ways of thinking. My quest for the secret to success did not reveal anything about the outside world. What it did do was reveal all the secrets I had within me. For within you, ladies and gents, is the secret to accomplishing your life dreams and goals. You are a masterpiece designed by your creator (whomever that may be to you; I call him God). You were created with the power of the universe and a creator essence inside.

You truly are all that you dream of becoming. All that you want to accomplish in life is already inside of you. There is no end to the universe, and there is no end to how far you can go in life. Look into your mind. What do you see? When I picture my mind, I see the universe. I see no beginning and no end. I see limitless power and potential. I see God. Most people that I have been around do not express their minds like that. For the longest time, I didn't. I am beyond grateful that I came to the realization that *I am All, I am That, I Am.* My purpose in life is to help people come to a similar realization about themselves. Look into your mind and break down the walls that say, "I am not smart enough, not beautiful or handsome enough. I am not tall, thin, white, or black enough." Break down the walls that say, "I was not born in the right situation. I have no money. It is not possible for me. Other people will not approve of it." Break all the walls and turn your mind into the universe. There is nothing that you cannot do. There is nothing that you cannot overcome, there is nothing you cannot forgive. Remember that Jesus even forgave those who crucified him. There is nothing that you cannot move on from if you attach yourself to time and move on with it. A limited mind will only equal a limited life.

I've rarely learned life-changing lessons from movies, but pay extremely close attention to the first *Kung Fu Panda*. In it, the dragon scroll was believed to contain secrets to limitless power. When the dragon warrior finally opened the dragon scroll, he was disappointed that it was blank. The only thing he could see was a reflection of himself. The scroll contained no secret, for all the dragon warrior had to do was look within and limitless power would be his. Millions of people saw that movie—kids, adults, black, white, rich, and poor. But how many people do you believe gained the knowledge but not a drop of wisdom?

Let's break down the difference between knowledge and wisdom and how the two are connected. Knowledge, as is defined in the dictionary, is "information gained through experience, reasoning, or acquaintance." Wisdom is defined as "the ability to discern or judge what is true, right, or lasting." For example, knowledge is that eating healthy food is better for your body; wisdom is choosing to eat it and to avoid unhealthy food. Information is all around us. Most of it nowadays is free (or very inexpensive). Libraries are full of books that you can use for free, Amazon.com sells thousands of the best books ever for less than ten dollars each, and

YouTube has a vast collection of audiobooks as well. If you are not careful, you could drown in information. But all information in the world doesn't do you any good without the wisdom to apply it.

We are not starving for information at this point. The wisdom within is what we lack. "Look within, look within" is something I have become accustomed to preaching, yet so many still do not understand the real meaning behind those words. Regardless of how I feel or what challenges I am facing in life, when I do not have the answers, the first thing I do is look within, and nine times out of ten, I get the answer. I can remember a few times when I simply was not happy for someone else's accomplishment, but then I looked within and realized that I was just not happy with myself. When I've been angry with someone, the best thing I have learned how to do is look within and find out what is going on. Almost instantly, I get the answer that enables me to move on and let go. To this day, I still doubt myself and make excuses, but I look within, and the answer for why I do those things comes to me.

On the positive side, when I am writing out my goals, I look within, and since I am the universe, there is nothing that I will not write if it is what I truly desire. I am able to quickly forgive when I look within. Issues that are life and death to most (or at least they act as if they are) are irrelevant to me because of my ability to look within. When you are able to look within and see the universe, then the biggest problems and the hardest challenges all of a sudden turn into tiny dots that you can easily step on and overcome. Even in writing this book, I often questioned if people would like this or that. Then I looked within and remembered that some people did not like Jesus. Approval is nice and beautiful, but by far, we do not need other people's approval to do what we want to do and become who we want to be.

My book will not appeal to everyone. It may change one person's life, while another person may find it a waste of time. My goal is to fulfill my purpose on this earth as Jesus fulfilled his and paid the ultimate cost. You were brought on earth for a purpose. You have all the tools, information, and help you wish to attract at your disposal. But most people never even seek to fulfill their purpose or even know they have one. The best thing you can do with your life is to give it back to the earth in such a way that other people are inspired by and benefit from it. Believe it or not, since the day you were born, you have been contributing to this earth. Whether it is in a positive or negative way is the part you have to figure out.

Whose life are you living? Have you accomplished what you were brought here to do? As long as you are alive, the answer to that question will always be no. Your work on this planet is done when your creator removes your soul from this life. You were not sent here to be unhappy, stressed, and unfulfilled. We often ask ourselves, why do birds stay in one place, for the most part? They have wings and can fly off to a rich neighborhood. We humans are a lot smarter and more capable than birds, yet we stay in the same bad relationship and work five days a week at the same job we hate while barely being able to pay rent. We live in the same house that we settled for due to the lack of belief that better is possible. We sit around like birds and simply accept what life has handed us. Most people's attitudes are what we see. What we have and who we are now is all that seems possible. That is why very few are truly successful. Most people defeat themselves before even trying. If it cannot easily be accomplished, then most people do not even bother considering it.

You are not most people, are you? After all, you made it this far in the book. Remember, you are the only secret that you will ever need to accomplish anything in life. Everything else on the outside is just information and technical things you must learn. Step one is getting to know that secret—get to know yourself, your mind and its way of thinking, your habits, and the principles you follow. Work on gaining knowledge and wisdom as if your life depends on it. Seek to be around those who have done the very thing you wish to do and learn from them. Learn from their mistakes, challenges, attitude, and so on. Learn their habits. I mentioned that I learned that successful people, those with passionate dreams and those who are hungry for more, usually wake up before 5:00 a.m. every morning. What is the advantage behind choosing to wake up that early? Everything you do is a choice, and your choices add up to the person you are. The people who complain about not having enough time are poor time managers. Twenty-four hours is more than enough time, and one of the best ways to maximize that time is to start your day early. Get up early and feed your mind, body, and soul before facing the outer world.

It is impossible to grow your outer life any bigger than your inner self. It does not matter how badly you might want to be a doctor, lawyer, teacher, businessperson, or president if you do not first work to expand your mind to do what you must do today to accomplish your goals tomorrow. Your dreams will be the ghost that you will have to face on your deathbed. The very few people who make it to the top without gaining the necessary knowledge and wisdom for the position usually fall back down. Luck can only take you so far.

What is the one thing I would like for you to get out of this book? Make every day of your life a day to learn, practice, and improve. It does not matter if you can only spare thirty minutes a day. Those minutes add up over time, and you will learn how to increase the time you have to invest in learning.

As I conclude this book, this meal, what is the one thing you know you should start working on immediately? What dreams and goals did you bury alive because of fear and self-doubt? What targets are you currently aiming for in your relationship, career, or personal life—and why? How will hitting those targets contribute to the world around you?

Reading books is one of the best things you can spend your time on. I see every book I read as a meal for the mind. My mind loves to eat, and yours does too. Remember, whether you select what you feed your mind or it eats something else, it does not care. I highly recommend reading. At this point, I can easily distinguish someone who reads from someone who doesn't. The differences in their attitude and mental processes are mind-blowing. The knowledge and the wisdom I have gained are something that no one can take away from me. You can lose your job, your house, your car, or your spouse—anything that is not within you can easily disappear in a heartbeat. It does not serve you to make material things part of who you are. That will only hold you hostage to the outside world. Be free and live from within.

CHAPTER 10
MY STORY

As I a write these words, I am twenty-seven years old. My goal is to be a published author before I am twenty-eight. I have failed at this before, but it didn't stop me. At this point, just being alive for another birthday is no longer a reason for me to celebrate. I want to celebrate because I am living, I am improving, I am accomplishing, and I am making the most out of my life and giving back. I aim to give back my life to the world. I love reading books, listening to audio programs, and watching people share their knowledge and stories on stage. Those things truly inspire me. It is crazy how someone else's words can change your life. My goal is to do the same with my message now. The only thing that is original on my end is my personal story and experiences. My teaching and my messages are lessons that have been around for thousands of years, yet few people seek out or practice any of them.

Every single year, I will accomplish a major goal that will serve as the reason to celebrate my birthday. And hopefully, long after this body is gone, that tradition can continue through my family and whoever has learned from my teaching. My story goes deep; my past pain, failures, and challenges I have had to overcome go even deeper than I can express in words. I have yet to meet a person who's faced more struggles than I have, though I am pretty sure that there are a number of them. We just have not yet had the pleasure of meeting. My pain, failures, and challenges played a major role in why today I aim to give my life back to the world as positively as I can.

My dark moments nearly drove me to my last breath more times than I can count, but God almighty had different plans for me, and today I am fulfilling those plans. I do not wish to share many negative stories here, for this book's aim is to feed the mind positively. But I have read negative stories that have inspired me to do better and to believe that no matter what my current failures are, I still can choose what I do next. Therefore, I will give you a glimpse of mine to show that I did not simply go to school, read books, and become able to write words like these. I have lived and overcome the challenges I faced. That is why today, I can truly say that no matter where you are in life right now, you can still make the best of it.

Say you're doing life in prison and are reading these words. Instead of being part of any negativity, you can devote your life to educate those who still have a shot at the outside life to do better. You can write books about your experiences in prison that may help promote fewer crimes. Your choices are many, but remember to keep it simple and figure out what you can do today to make the rest of your life the very best that it can possibly be. If I can come up with ideas for someone in prison for life, it should be simple for you to come up with endless ideas for your own life. My goal is to inspire millions by the time I take my last breath. If it has been done before, then it is possible for me to do it—simple as that. The road map to whatever you seek to be great at already exists. You just have to follow it.

And our youth is the future. My focus is to reach as many as possible. Many kids today are being raised in environments that cripple their minds and their futures unknowingly. I have seen videos on Facebook of bad parenting that have left me speechless. I do not care to judge, only to use my voice and knowledge to make a difference. I have witnessed on several occasions how people who are much older than I act as if they were twelve years old. Again, physical growth does not equal mental growth, and that is why today, I have dedicated my life not only to improve myself but as many other souls as possible.

Thousands of years ago, the majority were poor or average, and a few were wealthy and ruled others. Today, that has not truly changed. Most people are living average lifestyles, while few are wealthy and rule over the average masses. Yet so many people seem to believe that a new year also means "a new me." The year changes, but people and challenges in this life don't. The language is different. Technology and quality of life have improved, but we aren't living powerfully any more than those who came before us thousands of years ago. Assuming that change comes with time and new governments is a recipe for mediocrity. Real change comes from learning, practicing, and constant action.

I can look back as far as I can remember and add up the hows and whys that my life is the way it is today. I can add up why I failed so many times, why I was emotionally and mentally weak, why I never reached for anything past what my eyes were seeing. After all, seeing is believing, right? That is what I grew up hearing. Unfortunately, all I ever saw around me at best was a bunch of average people with no goals and no aim to live among the stars. My real struggle began when my marriage failed. That was the first time I tasted real failure. I did everything humanly possible to put the pieces back together, but I was alone in that. My former soul mate had moved on. I tried to win her with words, but I failed. I tried to win her with gifts. I even bought her a new ring, but I failed. I failed, I failed, and I failed. Meanwhile, I had to go to work every day as a US Marine, feeling like death on the inside but looking and acting like Superman on the outside. I was embarrassed and too ashamed to get the help I desperately needed.

Going home was a nightmare. I would unlock my front door, and my dog was no longer there to greet me. All the lights were off, as if the place had been abandoned. There was no smell of dinner, and no one to hold or talk to. I had been with this girl since I was fifteen. I was getting divorced at twenty-three, and now I had to learn how to breathe without her love. Needless to say, mentally and emotionally, I was in a coma. I worked the night shift, so even at work, I was alone with my thoughts, my pain, and my struggles. Life became a big nightmare with no end in sight. I popped pills to go to sleep and then turned around and used energy drinks to stay up. Somewhere in between the lines, I started not caring about my military career. After all, my world was over. Or at least, that is what it felt like.

After more than a year of living a life of lies and pain, my closet was full of skeletons. Then one day, I got the call...I was being investigated by the military. Just when I thought life could not get any worse, it did. I was going through a divorce that I had not wanted, I was fighting for my life emotionally every day, and now I was public enemy number one in my unit (and several other units who had heard about my skeletons; bad news travels faster than the speed of light). I went from sitting in meetings with the commanding officer and sergeant major to cleaning bathrooms and taking out the trash. I was a sergeant (E5), going from being in charge of assurance that my unit was training ready to doing working parties, which included duties such as cleaning, cutting grass, taking out crash, the tasks usually perform by jr. marines. To sum it up, I spent two years fighting for my dead marriage and was investigated by the Marine Corps during the second year of that fight. They all talked about me and judged me. There is not a bad word in the English dictionary that has not been said about me by a lot of people who only heard stories. The way my unit treated me was like spending three months in jail, yet I was only being investigated, not convicted. What I went through then I would not wish on anyone—not even Hitler. Yes, I just said that.

My divorce was finalized, and the military ended up prosecuting me for things that marines do every weekend. These were not crimes, just everyday life BS. No, I do not blame the military one bit or anyone else involved. My actions got my butt in that position, and the best thing I did was take full responsibility. In doing so, I learned more than I can put into words. Going through those experiences only made me stronger. They only helped me to become a better person, not a bitter one. I had been buried with no way out but suicide—or at least that's what I thought. When I began working on my mind, reading and listening to inspiring stories, and practicing their lessons, I realized that it was only one chapter in the book of my life and that I still had endless pages to write on. Instead of committing suicide like I had planned, I turned into a seed that grew. Now I possess a mind-set that I can't quite describe. My hunger for knowledge, success, and giving back to the world keeps me up at night and wakes me up before the sun daily.

I began losing my taste for a lot of things I had been doing. For example, I used to watch ESPN religiously. I knew what was going on in every major athlete's life. I used to understand the sports world as if I was being paid to. Watching ESPN was only costing me my most valuable asset: time. I am not suggesting that you shouldn't follow sports. I do suggest that it will do you more good to spend time working on you than keeping up with your favorite team or athletes. You will probably enjoy the game more anyway sitting courtside than in your living room. The more time you spend in front of the TV, the less likely you will take the opportunity to enjoy your favorite team up close and personal. Going to clubs also lost its shine. I don't want to wait in line to get into a crowded place and pay for overpriced drinks. Bill Gates is not doing that, so why should I?

My thinking changed dramatically over time. I began to ask myself questions like, "If Bill Gates was in my shoes right now, what would he be doing? Going to clubs or working on owning the club? When Bill Gates is with his friends, what does he talk about? Gossip? Who's dating whom? Or ideas about business and self-improvement? If Bill Gates had the option of buying the new Jordan shoes or the new book, which would he pick?" I studied the likes of Gates, President Obama, and many others. I am not where they are yet, but to get there, I have to start thinking and acting as if I already am. If you are waiting to be in the position you want before you start thinking and acting as if you are already there, then you will always be waiting. We must see ourselves in the future first way before we get there.

You can find inspiration all around you, but again, it goes back to your mind-set to recognize how you can turn the negatives that you see as fuel to push you toward getting better. Being raised poor in a bad neighborhood and having to watch your parents struggle can be a blessing and an inspiration. It is all about how your mind sees it. There is someone out there today being raised on next to nothing, but instead of letting that determine where he or she ends up in the world, that person can make a choice to do better and to have more—not just for him- or herself, but for parents and family.

Nowadays, I am inspired by a lot. My mind can find a blessing in the worst situation. But here are a few of my early inspirations. There's Dr. Eric Thomas, a.k.a. the Hip-Hop Preacher. The first motivational speech I ever heard was from this guy. The first book I bought was his. The first time I looked at life differently was after I heard him speak. And I have not looked back since. There's Les Brown. This man made me believe that I can. His story inspires me to bury all my excuses and all the reasons I'd been telling myself that I can't write books, speak on stage, or be a success. His passion and love for speaking and how he aims to inspire is truly remarkable. There's the late Dr. Wayne Dyer. His words are so deep and moving, and his style of teaching is extremely calm yet very powerful and effective. Every time I listen to Dr. Dyer, it feels as if my soul is being cleansed. I have learned wisdom from Dr. Dyer that has elevated me to new inspiration.

I am who I am because of my past, my struggles, and my failures, for they were blessings in disguise. Physically, people recognize me, but mentally I always hear, "Who are you?" from the people who know me best. Keep it simple. No matter what you're going through, no matter how impossible the challenges may seem, no matter how many times you get knocked down, no matter how many people turn their backs on you, no matter how dark the world may seem, always keep fighting. Always keep improving, and keep getting back up. As long as you are breathing, no human truly knows how far you can go, regardless of where you currently are in life. One life to live, one life to live, one life to live. You can either create that life; learn from your mistakes; overcome your fears, doubts, and challenges; and be a lifelong learner, or you can accept whatever crumbs you can get your hands on. Thank you for reading. I hope this book inspires you to start working on a better you this instant.

My Top Ten Books (All are available as audiobooks.)

1) *Think and Grow Rich*, by Napoleon Hill. Every time I read this book, I see something new. How is that possible? The book did not change, of course. I did.
2) *Outliers*, by Malcom Gladwell. This book slapped some reality into my life. I used to believe that successful people had to be geniuses or born with God-given talents until I read this book.
3) *How to Win Friends and Influence People*, by Dale Carnegie. Plain and simple, if you plan on being around people in your lifetime, this book is a must read.
4) *Who Moved My Cheese?* by Spencer Johnson. This book feels like something for kids, but the message behind it is something all adults needs to hear.
5) *Increase Your Financial IQ*, by Robert Kiyosaki. If you wish to be wealthy, then you have to study wealth.
6) *The E-Myth Revisited*, by Michael E. Gerber. If you are thinking about owning a business, this book might possibly save your life.
7) *The Magic of Thinking Big*, by David Schwartz. The title of this book literally speaks for itself.
8) *The 10X Rule*, by Grant Cardone. This book is pure gold. The 10X Rule, when applied in any area of life, will produce massive results.
9) *The Neuropsychology of Self-Discipline* audio sessions by Steve DeVore. This one made me realize why success kept eluding me, and I am sure it will do the same for you.
10) *Unlimited Power*, by Anthony Robbins. This book covers every aspect of life. There is too much knowledge and wisdom in this book to put into a brief description. It's a must read!

Made in the USA
San Bernardino, CA
27 October 2016